ANIMAL ICONS

Colouring Book

Isabelle Brent

Fish
Seahorse
Dragonfly
Butterfly
Frog
Snail
Duck
Hummingbird
Robin
Whale
Hare
Squirrel
Badger
Zebra
Fox
Gazelle
Rhinoceros
Elephant
Blue-Tits
Owl

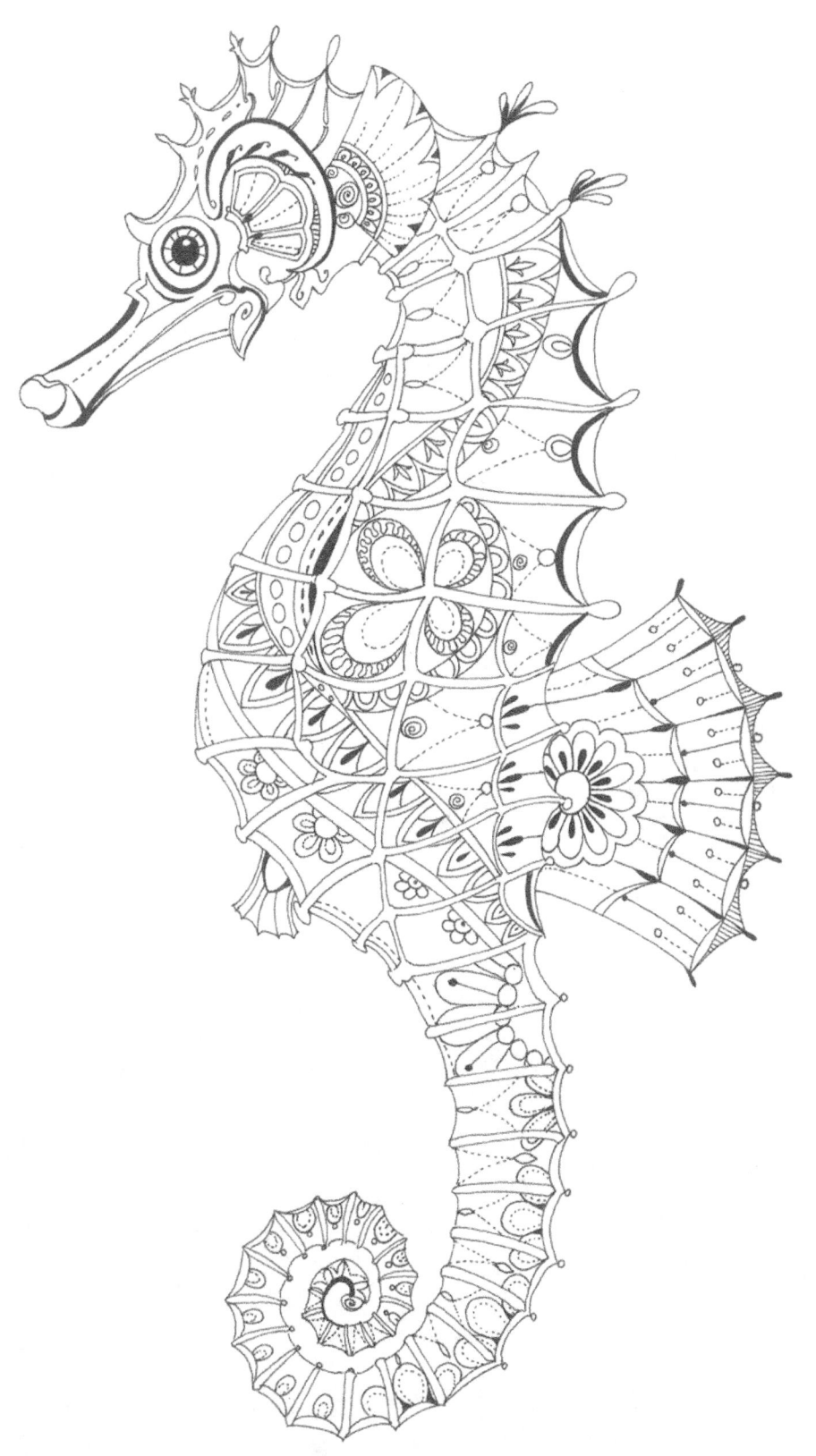

Pour mon Félix, qui a inspiré cette création.